Gateways

A Collection of Poems

John S. Langley

Copyright © 2023 J. S. Langley

The right of J. S. Langley to be identified as the Author of the Work has been asserted by him in accordance to the Copyrights, Designs and Patents Act 1988.
The Copyright for each poem resides with the author. All images are the property of the author or freely available in the public domain.

First Published in 2023 by LV Publishing

Apart from any use permitted under UK copyright law, this publication may only be reproduced, stored in a retrieval system, or transmitted, in any form, or by any means, with prior permission in writing of the publisher or, in the case of reprographic production, in accordance with the terms of licenses issued by the Copyright Licensing Agency.

All characters and events in this publication, other than those clearly in the public domain, are fictitious and any resemblance to real persons, living or dead, is purely coincidental.

Print ISBN: 978-1-7391381-6-5

Gateways

Now is a Gateway from yesterday
Now is a Gateway to tomorrow

A Gateway is something designed
to get through to the other side
A Gateway is meant to be used

This book is a Gateway from me
This book is a Gateway to me

Poetry is a Gateway to the soul.

John S. Langley

To Janet

CONTENTS

I. PERSONAL AND UNIVERSAL   Page

1.	The Magic of Marks	2
2.	Concentric Circles	4
3.	Which Loo	5
4.	Hear Me!	7
5.	Broken and Re-set	9
6.	Finding Out	12
7.	Dyslexia	14
8.	Film Club	15
9.	Best Mates	16
10.	Things I did to upset my Dad	17
11.	Missed Opportunities	20
12.	Unilever	21
13.	Border Crossing	22
14.	Intervention	24
15.	We Are The Medicated	26
16.	Bon Voyage	27
17.	Buying Ferraris	28
18.	Modern Circuses	30
19.	Look for the Joy	32
20.	Being teased by a Grandchild	33
21.	After a Visit	34
22.	Emotional Blackmail	35
23.	Diverted	38
24.	Observations	40
25.	Settle!	42
26.	Coming Home?	44

27.	Evie	46
28.	The Same Road?	48
29.	Men Leaf Fall	50
30.	Men	51
31.	Where Romans Walked	52
32.	Where Romans Walked – II	54
33.	Just a Tree?	56
34.	Boring	58
35.	River Kayaking	60
36.	Stacking Wood	62
37.	Hawthorns	64
38.	The Year of the Chilli	66
39.	Bread of Life	68
40.	A Tribute	70
41.	Ghost Light	71
42.	Reversal Selective Memory	72
43.	Reversal of Fortunes	74
44.	What Matters Most	76
45.	Reflections	78

II. **JUSTIFIABLE CONCERNS**

46.	Current Ego-systems	80
47.	Open up the Zoo	83
48.	An Ancient Pandemic	84
49.	A Modern Prayer	86
50.	A Balanced Argument?	87
51.	Telephone Warning	88
52.	Strike	90
53.	UNITY Acrostics	91
54.	Lost & Found	92
55.	Old Knowledge	94

56.	Standing Stones	96
57.	Antecedents	98
58.	Listening to the Ancestors	100
59.	Darn	102
60.	What if	104
61.	Carnivorous	106
62.	Layers	108
63.	The Naming of Parts	109
64.	A Bird Fable	110
65.	Pylons	111
66.	The Trouble with Parts	112
67.	AI	114
68.	What's in a name	115
69.	No-Brainer	116
70.	Seeing is Believing?	117
71.	Changes	118
72.	Categorisation	119
73.	The Missing Element	122
74.	Going Extinct	124
75.	Up in Smoke	126
76.	Climate Crisis	127
77.	Mutual Dependence	128
78.	The Problem Was	130
79.	The Difference	132
80.	Lost Cause?	133

III. NATURALLY SPEAKING

81.	Fleur de Leaf	136
82.	The Best Laid Plans	138
83.	Spring Yellow	140
84.	First Apples	141
85.	Go Sloe	142

86.	Blackberries	143
87.	Evidence	144
88.	A New Perspective	145
89.	Windhover	146
90.	Dragonfly	147
91.	And Away...	148
92.	The Hawthorn Ridge	150
93.	Empty Hive	152
94.	A Trifling Imperative	153
95.	Green Man?	154
96.	The Right Thing?	156
97.	Fireflies	157
98.	Perspectives	158
99.	Home?	159

IV. A FEW MORE

100.	Posser	164
101.	Proggy Mat	165
102.	Tankard	166
103.	Orkney Chair	168
104.	Loch Ness	170
105.	Hills	172
106.	19th Century Explorer	173
107.	Trains	174
108.	Never the Right Weather	175
109.	The Hubble Universe	176
110.	Cloud Cuckoo Land	178
111.	Green	179
112.	Inking	180
113.	It Would Have Been Superb!	184

Gateways

God grant me the patience
to accept the things I cannot change
the courage to change the things I can
and the wisdom to know the difference.

Gateways

God grant me the patience
to accept the things I cannot change
the courage to change the things I can
and the wisdom to know the difference.

PERSONAL AND UNIVERSAL

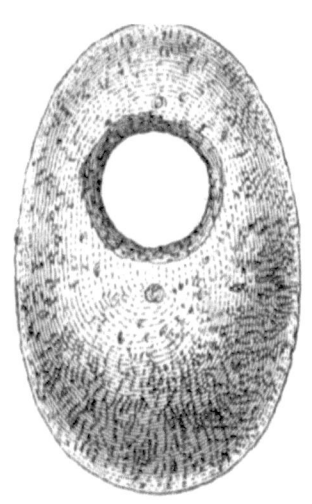

John S. Langley

The Magic of Marks

Ink upon a page
black upon white
a symbiosis of symbols

that through the Magic
of internalisation

become sounds

> **Ping, Pong, Crash...**

become colours

> **Red, Blue, Green...**

tell stories

> **Jack and the Beanstalk,**
> **Lord of the Rings,**
> **Atonement...**

from eye to brain
movies play
in the mind

If that's not Magic
what is !?

Gateways

John S. Langley

Concentric Circles

Me
  Family
Close Friends
        Friends
          Colleagues
         Acquaintances
           Everyone Else

           Everyone Else
         Acquaintances
          Colleagues
        Friends
Close Friends
  Family
Me

Gateways

Which Loo

As soon as I was old enough
to notice
I told my Mum I needed to go
to the boy's loo

But my Mum was clever
and she pointed
to a sign and said, 'Look
what it says'

I looked, 'It says Lad-dies,' she said
'it's a special loo
for little lads just like you.'
'Then why, Mum,'

I asked, 'do you always come
in with me?'
'Because I want to look after
you, that's what

Mum's do.' 'OK,' I said, 'then
why do some
women go in on their own?'
She thought

and then she said, 'They're
practicing.'
I was now content with these
answers

'OK, Mum,' I said, 'let's go.'
And even
to this day when I see a
'Ladies' loo

I remember how clever
Mothers are.

Hear Me!

A seven year old can't hear
His ears full of compacted wax
Can't understand how others
Can answer the teacher
When he can't hear the question

The teacher thinks he is messing
Shifts him to the back of the class
Writes him off as only a dunce
Who doesn't listen, who doesn't
Understand the simplest things

A mother hears of this judgement
Asks her son what's going on
He answers as best as a 7 year
Old can, thinks his sensory world
Is the same as everyone else's

Can't understand why others hear
He must be a dunce as teacher says
It's the only possible explanation.
His mother leaves him to play then
Creeps up behind him and whispers

He continues to play. Does not hear.
He is taken to the Doctor who looks
Into his ears and can see nothing but
Wax. He tells the parents and charges
Up an ear syringe with warm water

An enamel tray is held below the left
Ear to catch discharges. The syringe
Is inserted, the handle pushed; who-
Osh! Clank! A bullet hard sphere of
Brown-yellow wax lands in the tray…

The exercise is repeated on the right
Ear with the same result. 'How's that?'
Says the doctor. The boy clamps his
Hands over his ears 'Stop shouting!'
The world has become overwhelming

Too noisy to bear. 'Put cotton wool in
His ears, it will take a few days for him
To adjust.' And they do. And he does.
14 years later he leaves University
With a First Class Honours Degree.

Moral:
Don't write children off too early
They might surprise you!

Broken and Re-set

In one moment
rushing in from the garden
having been called in for tea
I tripped

A simple thing
my left leg got twisted under me
all my weight and speed turned to
instant pain

My father complained I was putting it on
hauled me up, told me to come
to the table

I couldn't walk, my mother saw it was real
put warm water in the washing up bowl
bathed the leg

When she saw the bone sticking out
she called my father over and they
rushed me to hospital

The drive was a nightmare, every bump
a new excruciating pain. I think I went
unconscious

John S. Langley

The X-Ray showed a double fracture
of the femur. I was in plaster 9 months
from hip to toe

I couldn't go to school. I once went back
in a wheelchair for people to sign my plaster
with names and wishes

I missed too much and was dumped from A
to C and left to fill up the teacher's inkwells
Red and Black

Later I was gifted a chance in the B class after
complaints to the headmaster
from my parents

I fell in love with Mrs Trotter who was nice
to me and clawed my way up to the A class
just in time

for the 11-plus. I think I got some home tuition
I can't remember, but somehow enough of the
gap was closed

Thank goodness I did not understand the
importance of the exam. Had a mock and
then the real thing

Gateways

I remember how anxious my parents were
I couldn't understand the concern, they'd
told me it didn't

matter if I passed or failed, I just had to do
my best. But that didn't seem to be the case
when the letter arrived…

        …that determined my future.

Finding Out

Thank you Enid Blyton
for the Five Find-outers
from a young boy who
was slow to read

Thank you Frederick
Larry, Daisy, Pip and Bets
and Buster the dog
of Peterswood

All 15 Mystery books
from Burnt Cottage
to Banshee Towers
read from cover to

cover - the first took
a week, the last less
than a day. Not bad
for a dyslexic!

Gateways

Dyslexia

Damned by a word that I cannot spell
You might think it funny but it's not
Sentenced as a simpleton to sit
Like a leper at the back of the class
Entertaining myself by looking at the
X's where there should be ticks. Labelled
Ignorant. Well hear this all of you, I
Am not stupid. And neither are the rest of us!

Film Club

When I was young there was
a Saturday morning film club
at the local Cinema

My father would generously
provide my brother and I the
sixpence needed

to gain entry. It was not until
much later I realised why my
parents might want

some time alone. We used to
queue to watch a full program
of Pathé News

Flash Gordon, a 'Road' movie
with Bing and Bob and a main
feature film

In the dark the light beamed
overhead full of dust motes
and fascination

It was not quiet, we cheered
the hero, booed the baddie
yeughed the kiss

and when we got home my
father was wearing a cravat
and smiling.

John S. Langley

Best Mates

Everybody needs best mates
to see them through their teens
I certainly did, my best mates
were; Maccy, Goody, Jock, Ed
with GG on the periphery

We had some experiences;
bounced from a night club for
dancing too flamboyantly,
sleeping on the street outside
St James' Park to get a ticket

for an FA Cup Semifinal against
Burnley, navigating the unknown
territory of girls, mainly without
success, playing football, sharing
the turbulent years of puberty

I still believe that if I were ever in
serious need I could ring any one
of my mates and they would be
there to help or, for that matter,
they could ring me.

Things I did that upset my Dad

Being born too late:
2 weeks overdue when
his holiday was up and
he was back at work.
I couldn't help it.

Turning a family picture
to the wall when I'd been
bed bound with a broken
leg for 6 weeks and was
going insane.
I was sorry I did this.

Not confessing when a
neighbour accused me
of repeatedly invading
his garden to retrieve a
football and I knew that
it wasn't me.
***I took the rap even though
I didn't do it.***

Getting only "Satisfactory"
for 'Conduct' on a school
annual report.
Fair enough - mea culpa.

John S. Langley

Supporting England and not
Scotland in any form of
competition.
*Yes, true. He would be doubly
upset if England won, as they
often did.*

Arguing about whether an
actor was Warren Mitchell
or Donald Pleasence
*I still don't know what the
fuss was about?*

Asking him to come and
give me a lift home when
I'd missed the last bus.
He'd just come in from work
and the mate I was with was
very drunk.
*I never asked him again. I'd
have rather curled up in a
ditch and died or crawled
home on my hands and knees
than suffer that humiliation
again!*

Gateways

Picking the wrong girl to marry!
*But to give him his due he
changed his mind and came
to treat her like a daughter.
They got on very well.*

Giving him a hug whether he
wanted one or not.
*Men of his generation did not
hug. But he got used to it.
After all, we're all human.*

Missed Opportunities

I wish I had
I could have if I'd wanted
It's too late now

When I was young
someone told me
"If you get an opportunity

treat it like it was the only
one. You may never
get another."

There are many things
I should have listened to
but I listened to this

and it's served me well.

Unilever

I worked for Unilever for nearly two decades.
I still carry a fondness of memory.

Started by an entrepreneur and family
the heritage is now in the hands of
different employees

The family long gone from presiding
Interest. It is the long serving workers
who watch over it

Pride in membership of an organisation
whose ambition to profit was balanced
by a measure of philanthropy

An ethos embraced by generations, the
pill swallowed whole, a lifetime of stable
employment on offer

More volatile now, as the world of work
changed so much, loyalty much less of
a valuable virtue

though there are still those friendships
forged through both good and bad
that maintain a connection

no matter what we've done since…

John S. Langley

Border Crossing

We cross the border on a blustery day
yet there is no border here
no line, no checkpoint, no fence
no mark upon the ground

Nevertheless my father, a son
of Lossiemouth, demands we stop.
He only wants to look, he says
to breathe the sweet-scented air.

Though I do not believe him, I stop.
I've known him all my life. I know
he will disobey all medical advice
and will do whatever he wants.

I close my eyes to avoid my guilt
by association. When I open them
he is outside. He has tottered through
bracken, found a springy purple spot

and has lain doon, not tripped or fallen
and is rolling in the Scottish heather.
I can hear him laughing and singing
and I try to ignore the absurdity of it all.

We have crossed a border this blustery day
even though there is no border here
no line, no checkpoint, no fence
no mark upon the ground.

Gateways

Intervention

Crazy paving covers the windscreen
Temperatures below freezing
The smoothness of toughened glass
The differential temperature inside to out
has sucked moisture from the laden air
and created this interlaced artwork of tendrils
fingers of ice reaching to cover the surface
blocking our view.

But we must leave and so
the scrapers are out, the antifreeze
is sprayed, the car engine is started
the heaters are on, blowers roaring
and directed at the inside of the glass.
All of this to reverse the frosting process
break the ice's hold, shift translucence
to transparency. The heat, chemical
and physical forces trying to win
the battle for visibility.

We get in the car, close the doors
cocoon, separate ourselves
once again from the outside world.
Our latest intervention complete
we switch on the heated seats
engage gear …

                     … and begin to move off.

Gateways

John S. Langley

We Are The Medicated

We are the medicated
We take pills for this and that
I'm going for a top up
I don't have time to chat

When we go to the Doctor's
With aches and pains and such
We get a new prescription
And still have time to lunch

Oh, we rattle in the mornings
Must drink to get them down
And try to recall their silly names
As we bus pass into town

Yes, we are the medicated
There are pills for everything
From obesity to loneliness
Don't worry about a thing

And when, in the final reckoning
The last prescription's filled
Just remember we last longer
Than our ancestors ever did

Bon Voyage

Stiff upper lip
Keep strong for the wife
It's the hardest thing
In the whole of my life

I wish you adieu
You'd better run
Goodbye and good luck
Go get 'em my son

Try not to forget us
Tho' we'll get along
And if you're ever in need
You know where to come.

Buying Ferraris

I've always wanted a Ferrari
I got sold on the glamour
and the hype

It's the sleek design lines
the red, the prancing horse
the whole thing

They say it costs £200,000
to raise a child in the UK
That's a Ferrari!

But when I actually got
to drive a Ferrari
around Silverstone

for 3 laps, it was enough
for me to realise
it was too small

or I'm too big
to fit comfortably and
I think that's important

Gateways

So I bought a home phone
shaped like a red Ferrari
to call the kids

now grown, partnered up
families of their own
and tell them

they are our Ferraris
that they're much better
than a car

and have appreciated in
value whereas a Ferrari's
value doesn't

To be honest their reaction
was mixed, but that's the
thing about kids

they say what they mean !

John S. Langley

Modern Circuses

We travel hundreds of miles
to watch a game, to shout
cheer or boo, to support
"our" team and when a player
thanks the fans we think they
are speaking personally to us
that we know each other well
even though we've never met
and if we did it could be a bit
awkward.

Why do we do it? What primal
need is satisfied by being part
of a baying tribe, dressing in
team colours, expecting only
the best, accepting the worst?
Is it our thirst for competition
our baser instincts to gather
as social animals and get lost
in the crowd?

To those of you who don't
understand, who can't see
the fascination in watching
people kick around a bag of
wind or throw one or hit one
with a racket, or a bat and not

Gateways

blanch at the sponsorship
the business sport has become
the astronomical salaries
paid to some, who instead of
being reproached are idolised
by millions, lauded like
demi-gods, I say this…

I don't understand it either
but I still do it!!

John S. Langley

Look for the Joy

Try to look for the Joy in things
my mother said
as she was preparing to die

This morning there were so many
beautiful birds
feeding in our garden

They made such a marvellous noise
chattering away
so full of life and song

That's what I tried to teach your father
after his stroke
put aside your anger and hunt for Joy

He had seen too much to talk about
in the War
it festered and bubbled inside him

It is the easiest and most difficult thing
Look for all those little joys
and celebrate them.

Gateways

Being teased by a Grandchild

Can you think of a word
that rhymes with cat?
No, not dog, but I can
see what you're thinking.

Can you think of a word
that you really like?
Well, you could say dog
but I'm not sure why.

Can you think of a word
that rhymes with log?
So now you say cat and
you're laughing at that!

I'm pleased I'm not your
teacher, what a handful you are
Yes, you can stroke the cat
I've decided to call it 'Dog'

I guess we're just chips
off the same block.

John S. Langley

After a Visit

Going back and worn out
Happy and sad together

Pleased that we came
Pleased we were here

the pain of parting
a familiar part

We dull the departure
with 'see-you-agains'

Not knowing
if or when

Life is made of memories
A jigsaw of many pieces

without a picture
as a guide

Today we have added
a corner fragment

and hope there'll be other
pieces to find

Emotional Blackmail

A composite conversation from eavesdropping others!

You're going on holiday?
Can't remember the last time
I had a holiday

It was a month ago

That wasn't a holiday
that was an escape
just for two weeks

I need a holiday!

You go then
don't worry about me
I'll be OK

I had to look after
my parents, you know
it was expected

After everything
they'd done
for me

But don't you worry
you go away
I'm sure I'll survive

somehow.
Enjoy your holiday
have a nice time

send me a postcard
if you can
be bothered

I have to go now

Yes, yes, you've
hardly been here
a moment

but off you go
I'm sure you've
more important

things to do.
Will I see you
tomorrow?

Yes

Gateways

Then, if you can
will you bring me
some Yorkshire tea

Yes, Mum

And some of those
nice biscuits
your Dad liked

Yes, Mum

Off you go now
I'll be alright
I always try

not to be a bother.
It's nice to talk to
you now and again

I'm not getting
any younger
you know.

John S. Langley

Diverted

The road is closed
It is night
The air is full of rain
The lanes are full of cars
The SatNav is confused
And so are we

Now we must follow
the yellow signs
with black lettering
through the smeared
windscreen, drive the
strange roads

We come to a roundabout
halfway round there is a sign
two actually
both saying 'Diverted Traffic'
with arrows pointing
in different directions !

What chance do you stand?

We took a chance
Stopped at a Service Station
Had a coffee
Used our smartphone
To find a way home

Gateways

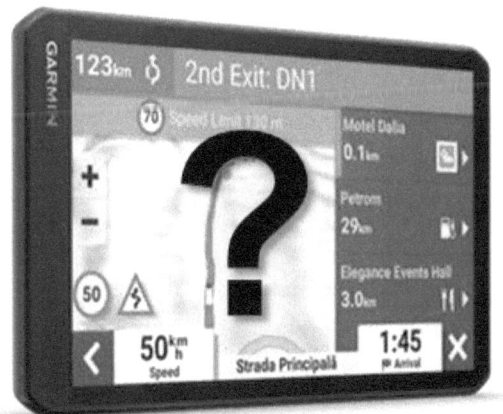

Observations

We are hardwired
to ignore our own mortality
though we see others go

For without this
we would miss moments of joy
or heartache
that is the bread of life

Like the sound of a blackbird singing
Like the sight of a lamb frolicking in the field
Like a cow standing with soulful eyes
chewing the cud
belching out methane

Like a multi-veined rainbow after rain
streaking it's arched bridge of colour
across the dome of the sky

Like watching a dolphin breach the surface
it's grey back flashing with reflected light
before it plunges back into the surf
to swim the unseen currents

Gateways

Like a swallow swooping
Like a blossoming rose
Like a summer sunset
Like the smell of damp hay

Like my Mother asking if I
at the age of 4, could see
the love light shining
behind her eyes

Like me returning to play
with toy soldiers
wondering why my Mother
seemed to be crying.

John S. Langley

Settle!

What is going on in my head ?
I just can't seem to settle
Too many things and too few
are jostling to join in the queue
of all the things I think I must do

But what if I didn't ?
What if I stopped and curled up
with a really, really 'good book'
or opened the door and went out
and took a much longer look?

Would the world stop turning?
Would the tides cease to be?
Of course not
nothing important
depends upon me

And maybe that's the problem
when you realise you're so small
all the things you think that matter
don't matter much at all

Gateways

You think you're in the middle
when you're very probably not
so perhaps the best solution
is to be grateful
for what you've got

I think that I might try it
I'll surely give it a go
and then my mind might settle
I'm really hoping so.

John S. Langley

Coming Home?

Sitting round an African campfire
freshly collected wood crackling
yellow-red flames licking upwards
to join a night sky littered with stars

At your back the blackness of an
African night, away from streetlights
away from towns, a circle of tents
and we, feeling not quite safe

yet somehow at home.

At such a time a calmness embraces
the group like a warm shawl and after
food, after drink, after preparing for
the night, we watch the fire, listen to

the night calls and let our talk turn
to life, experiences, hopes, dreams
as naturally as if we had known each
other for many years. This is the

Gateways

magic of this place, a soul magic that
seeps through your pores and into your
being, touching your mind, your body
your heart while, in a state of heightened

awareness of the surroundings, your
senses strain to listen, aware that not
all is secure, ready to react should the
circle be threatened or broken.

I do not remember what was said
I do not remember all the people's names
But what I do remember is that feeling
of belonging in a place
              I had never been to before.

Evie

'Hi, I'm Evie, what's your name?'
I told her

I met Evie at the toaster
part of a hotel buffet breakfast

'Even great men make mistakes,'
she said, 'I'm going to big school
next month and I'm a bit scared.'

'Don't be scared,' I said
parental protection clicking in

'I've never used a toaster before,' she said

'They're not easy,' I said, 'very temperamental
you either need to do it three times
or else it burns to a crisp.'

'Oh,' she said

And I realised my mistake

Gateways

'I'm sure this one will be OK,' I said
'and anyway I'll stay until it pops.'

'Thanks, my Dad will be worried
if I'm not back soon.'

The toaster popped
The toast was underdone

'Perfect,' she said
'Well done,' I said

She put the bread on a plate
picked up two gold-wrapped
pats of butter
and left

A passing acquaintance
but Evie made an impression

And after she'd gone
I wished her echo well

I still do.

John S. Langley

The Same Road?

I've been this way many times
stopped to talk for too long
about tups and yows and foot-rot
the state of the economy
the weather, how late
the swallows are

'It's a good'un today,' I say
but there is no reply
I talk into an empty space
and to myself

There are no new walkers
instead I dodge the silent
cyclists who approach
too fast from behind
with earpieces in
and sweat on their brow

Or step onto the verge
flattening the green grass
holding onto a fence post
avoiding the barbed wire
to let a speeding delivery van
swoosh past with a wave

Gateways

Everybody else seems to be
rushing to get from A to B
while I've stepped out
of the race
for a short space

Don't get me wrong
I'm no hero
I will rejoin
but in the meantime
I miss our chats
though the flies still circle
and the sheep still look on.

John S. Langley

Leaf Fall

A dried leaf skitters
Along a tarmac road
Driven by unseen forces
Alive as it dances with
It's curled brown edges
It's green heart

What does it signify?
Changing seasons
The end of something
The beginning of…
A fleeting moment
Nothing ?

I continue walking
There are many leaves
They fall all around me
The wind blows
and I move on.

Gateways

Men

I met a man upon the road
a fellow walker

We talked of cameras and
how birds don't stay still

I told him that there were
fewer swallows this year

He agreed and blamed
Global warming

We parted company.

I did not ask his name
nor he mine

We went our separate ways
none the wiser

But I remember this brief
meeting on the trail

Though I will not go
that way again.

John S. Langley

Where Romans Walked

I walk where Romans have walked
Though they would have given me
short shrift, if we had met

I could have tried to tell them
of all I had learnt from books and
films, and a really good tv show
about their lives

But they would not have understood
speaking a different language
and if they had replied, then I
would have been none the wiser

They would see me as a stranger
and I, strange in their strange world

If I had instead met, out in the open
a meat-eating dinosaur with nowhere
left to run my chances of survival
would be about the same!

Gateways

John S. Langley

Where Romans Walked - II
(or Enjoying the Countryside)

I walk where Romans have walked
dodging campervans

The Latin surface is buried beneath
a tarmac skin, in need of repair

It is tourist time
and I am asked for directions
to Birdoswald
or Housesteads
or the nearest Starbucks

The cyclists are deadly
in their silent running
three abreast
headcams on
brakes off

I hear echoes of feet
that will follow mine
Unknown lives
that must take their stride

Gateways

on whatever road they make
in whatever air we leave
but with what mind
hurrying to what harvest time ?

I just came out for a walk
to enjoy the peace
of this place
To mentally commune
with my surroundings
so small in a giant Universe

Not a chance!
It is too busy
I'd be better off
retreating indoors
making a coffee
and watching David Attenborough…

John S. Langley

Just a Tree?

On the morning of September 28th 2023 the 200+ year old tree that stood in 'Sycamore Gap' on Hadrian's Wall was found to have been felled, taken down by a chainsaw sometime during the night. As well as a brutal and thoughtless act of vandalism the loss of this iconic symbol of survival has brought sadness to many, including myself.

It stood there all my life
against the odds, filling a gap

Each time I passed on foot
or by car there was a nod

of familiarity, of fellowship
If there was one thing I felt

was secure. One thing I felt
I could rely on it was that tree.

Such a simple thing that asked
nothing of us but to leave it alone.

But even that simple request
symbolic of Nature's plight we

did not keep. And inside, down
to the very heart, that sycamore

Gateways

showed, when chainsaw felled it
in the night, that it was fit to live

for another hundred years or more.
It should have outlived me

It deserved to remain.
What harm was it doing?

What simple joy it brought into
so many lives. I am so sorry

that is all I can say, I am so sorry
so sorry…

John S. Langley

Boring

People ask isn't it boring
to walk the same road day after day
but yesterday I saw a flock of long-tail tits
the day before a Robin joined me on my walk
today a Crow caws noisily overhead and
I know that in a few weeks there will be
Redwings and Fieldfares feasting on the
Hawthorn berries.

The other day dragonflies were everywhere
red, blue hawkers and darters and larger
green-brown ones coursing the verges like
aerial dinosaurs in ancient gyroscopic display
In spring, there are lambs cavorting around
the field or suckling from their mothers and
at other times there are cows with calves and
the bellow of the bull

And I meet people on the walk
dog walkers, lost tourists, hikers, cyclists who
nearly take me out and people who stop their
cars for a chat. And I have time to remember
others who I used to meet and who talked to
me about tups and yows and foot-rot whose
lives were very different to mine but who were
willing to share their experiences

Gateways

and spare me some precious time from out
their working day. Then there is the peace
the clean air, the closeness to green, the ever
changing sky, the colours and textures of clouds
that fly or flit or dawdle in changeable weather
never knowing quite which clothes to wear for
the heat, the wet, or the breezy, dry leaves
crunching underfoot

freshly fallen, blown from adjacent trees
majestic in their age, bark deep wrinkled their
bases green with moss. And this year there were
butterflies in white and browns, and a mass of
Red Admirals fluttering, their black wings slashed
with red and white, settling on roadside blooms
and overhead the swallows and martins flew like
arrows amidst a buzzard's call

So no, I don't find it boring.

John S. Langley

River Kayaking

Seeing life
at water level
the only sound
a dipping paddle
the chatter of birds
the reeds swaying
by the bank
No Alice here to
see a rabbit, only
a reflected sky
and milky moon
to preside over
these moments
of solace
of peace
a sense of place
being in

Gateways

being part of
as words disappear
like ripples
to the soft sound
of the keel
slicing through
a crystal surface …
…………….
………..
……
…
.

John S. Langley

Stacking Wood

Is an art form
soft or hard
separated
layered
to make
identification
easier
later
in the snow

But now
on arrival
what matters
is emptying
the haphazard
bags
storing it
properly
to keep it dry

Gloves on to
avoid spelks
a conveyor
of passing logs
then placing
repeat…

Gateways

A job to do
A need to satisfy
A talent to show
A prospective entry
for the Turner Prize

Look on ye sceptical
and be amazed!

John S. Langley

Hawthorns

I have to admit
that I don't like hawthorns
though they seem to love me

Once a year
we have to cut them back
or else they just take over

Thick leather
oven gloves we've found
avoid permanent damage

Though you
can't avoid getting
an odd scratch or two

Once a year
is enough! Even though
their bright red berries

Gateways

are essential
to feed our migrant
wintering birds. I just

wish they'd
learn from the rowan
and not be so lethal!

John S. Langley

The Year of the Chilli

This year was the year of the chilli

Last year was the year of the giant onion
larger than any onion I'd ever grown.
It was a big success

This year it was the turn of the chilli.
I'd never grown them successfully before
so I hedged my bets

and tried three different ways; seeds
plants from an online seedling supplier
and a local garden centre

The first seeds failed. I tried again.
The second pack germinated and grew
painfully slowly

some were attacked by persistent aphids
others faded away, some survived and
produced flowers

All three experiments produced chillis
and it was interesting to watch the transition
from green to red

Gateways

the opposite to waiting on traffic lights.
Now I have too many chillis
of three varieties

that I've lost the labels for!
We're trying them, carefully
in omelettes, in curries, in chutney
and a strange smelling sauce.

I think I can say it's been a success
Some are quite hot!
Now the big question is
what will next year be the year of?

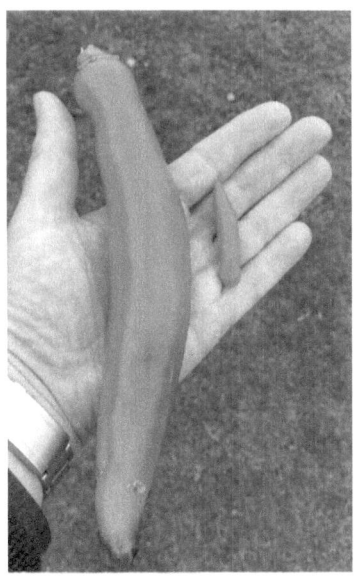

John S. Langley

Bread of Life

What is the world coming to
When stottie cakes arrive
Through the Post !?

Fresh baked that morning
Couriered in a cardboard box
Wrapped for freshness

Opening the parcel is like
Peeling back the years
To a forgotten youth

Rekindled by the smell, the
Soft interior, the browned
Outside that I tap

With a knuckle and listen
For the echo of former days
In a mother's kitchen

Full of never-ending chores

They are the real thing these stotties
Buttered thick, spread with pease pudding

Gateways

Layered with Slices of ham
I savour them

And afterwards
I turn away
The wind in my eye

Pick up my iPad
And contemplate
Placing another order.

John S. Langley

A Tribute

Here's a tribute to a friend of mine
Who said all poetry had to rhyme
He argued only in this way
Could the written word hold sway

I said, 'What about T. S. Eliot?'
He said, 'Who, can you spell-it?'
I said, 'Is it one "t" or is it two?'
He said, 'I don't know, I asked you!'

And so we'd go back and forth
That's what we do, here in the North
We'd never agree, but so what
At least we'd never lose the plot

What mattered most was that we cared
And most of all were never scared
To say what we thought, argue a point
Cos at least our feeling for poetry was joint.

Gateways

Ghost Light

Light from an infant star, white
as a schoolboy's lie, competing
forces seeking a stable
maturity through fusion

a middle age that yields
much heat and light, chasing
its firstborn through the ether
never to catch it. Finally, fuel depleted

it pulses towards extinction while
that first light reaches my eye
in my short now. A memory, a ghost
light, far from its source that

is no more, whose explosively
expelled dust has joined with other
matter and, in time, may become part
of fresh offspring, sparking into life

a new light emitted
a fresh cycle begun.

John S. Langley

Selective Memory

Why can I remember
as if it were yesterday
my new brother being
brought home
when I was only 3

Or my youngest brother
when I was 10
but I can't remember
what I did last week
even when I should!

What is it about my brain
that captures some
things but rejects others?
Choices I appear to
have no control over

I can remember 'pass the
parcel' at my 8th birthday
party (I didn't win) but
I can't remember where
I left my phone

Gateways

The only positive
is that I probably
won't remember
writing this poem
so should I come across it

sometime later
it'll be like
reading something
that was written
by somebody else.

Reversal of Fortunes

Everything seemed to be intent
on becoming a disaster.

Nothing was going right
Whatever I tried went wrong:

I made a coffee and spilt it
I locked myself out of the car
I forgot an appointment…

I was getting exasperated
I was thinking today must be
my biorhythm's triple low

… and then the phone rang
and it was you

I was delighted and
within 5 minutes my
problems seemed small

Gateways

my day just got better
and afterwards:

I found my spare car keys
I made a new appointment
I made myself a coffee

… and did not spill it

It's amazing how little
it can take
to cheer you up!

What Matters Most

'What matters most,' she said
'is to have had love in your life.
It's much more important than
money.'

I was ear-wigging a conversation
very bad manners I know, but
what this lady was saying seemed
important

'There are those,' she continued
'who believe they have bought the
right to be obnoxious with impunity
but they haven't.'

I thought about this for a moment
Does the acquisition of wealth or
class confer special privileges
such as this?

'We might choose to put up with
it,' she said, 'because it doesn't
really matter, what matters is to
have love in your life.'

Gateways

'If you have love, you see these
things for what they are, they are
nothing compared to love, so look
to yourself, and love.'

This was a deep conversation to
happen upon. I stuck around and
apologised for over-hearing such
personal talk

'Oh,' she said, 'I didn't notice you.
Don't worry, he was feeling bad.
I was just trying to put things
in perspective.'

'Do you believe it?' I asked, 'Do
you believe what you said?' She
smiled, 'I've been very lucky, I've
had love in my life

and now, when I look back, it's
the only thing I remember that
really matters. Now how can
I help you?'

'You already have,' I said.

John S. Langley

Reflections

How did you spend those hours?
Now that they're used up
Like savings on a rainy day
Irrecoverable. Depleted.

Did you do the things you wanted to?
When you ran down the backstreets
arms spread wide, feet splashing
struggling to get airborne.

Was the world as wild as you thought?
Listening in class, reading from books
waiting in airports, going to places
you'd never been.

And was home the same when you came back?
Had the shops closed, the grass grown taller
burying your youth underfoot, adding
another layer to the hidden strata.

You ask "What about you?" and out of the blue
I am transported back on outstretched arms
and racing feet to times both fun and teary
I pause. "I asked you first," I say.

Gateways

JUSTIFIABLE CONCERNS

John S. Langley

Current Ego-systems

Reality TV brings together
exaggerated ego-systems
egged on by Producers
who feed on the number
of Social Media hits

Marriage ceremonies are sold
to the highest bidder
and held inside
security cordons at
the level of Fort Knox

All phones
are taken in at the gate
with no exceptions

The stakes are too high
for the Brands
that have paid to supply
the clothes, the jewels
the food, the perfumes and cosmetics
for all of the sexes.

Gateways

Media-fuelled expectation
attracts gossip circulation sales
like iron filings that obey
the laws of Physics and follow
the magnetic lines of force

In a world where
everyone loves everyone
unless a public feud
is more effective
every little thing is done
to protect popular perception

The commentator's curse
must not derail
today's gravy train
that brings big bucks
and the adulation
of the markets
in conspiratorial profiteering

And when interest levels decline
a collision of egos
is contrived

John S. Langley

by smart agents or publicists
designed to create
gravity waves
that course through the internet
like an AI driven tsunami
creating chaos
creating interest
making money
out of a fleeting burst
of viral indignation

Most of these ego-systems
have a short shelf life
are easy reading
in a world in need of distraction
easily forgotten role models
who we manufacture
with wrinkle free smiles
live in the light of the public eye
until they are eclipsed
by the next big sensation
ready for their time in the Sun.

Gateways

Open up the Zoo

I think we should
Lock up all the leaders
Down in London Zoo
Let them tell the alligators
What they're going to do

Talk to the Orangutan
And help him understand
How cutting down his food
Is an inevitable consequence
of supply and of demand

Let them tell the snakes
That they shouldn't hiss
Because things are pretty good
And could be worse than this

Lock up all the gates
And throw away the key
Let them fight to survive
When the animals are free

John S. Langley

An Ancient Pandemic

Only 3,000 years ago
the first human pandemic
was detected as a virus
residing in electrum
in a place now part of Turkey.

The Romans then spread it
from the temple of Juno Moneta
mixing religion with the infection
ensuring the lack of antidotes
so that every culture in every part

of the world was unable to
combat the invasion of
this parasitic incubation that
pierced their lives to the core
determining their choices.

And so it is to this day
this virus we all carry
inculcated into our DNA
so deep that we all want to know
'How much money do you make?

Gateways

A Modern Prayer

My money is safe in a haven
Hallowed is its fame
My income secure
My future assured
Purchasing anything under the Sun

Give me each day more than I can spend
And separate me from the masses
As I ignore them
That seek to annoy me

And lead me to all temptations
Avoiding much that is illegal
For mine is this kingdom
My power is my glory
Through endeavour I am clever
forever and forever
Amen

Gateways

A Balanced Argument?

A public outcry
based on half truths
and half-baked stories
becomes accepted fact
in less than a week
of headlines

Hours of airtime are given
to repetitious accusations
'There's No smoke without fire'
seems to be the natural law
of ambitious journalism

People listen to what
they want to hear and ears
are open to the news
of the next disaster

Little good news is reported
it doesn't make good TV
or radio, online or print

And if the allegations prove
to be unfounded then whisper

<small>it in the small print</small>

        … and carry on regardless…

John S. Langley

Telephone Warning

The telephone rings
I'm about to be arrested
My computer is compromised
My bank account has been invaded
I must listen and be persuaded

The voice is calm though accented
Wishing only to be helpful
I just need to do what I'm told
to sort out this obvious error

Now can I just please confirm
my name, my age, my bank
my credit card, my savings
and they'll go and sort it out

They advise that I keep quiet
don't tell anyone about this call
after all I don't want to risk
damaging my reputation

I thank them for their efforts
but decline their proffered help
with electricity prices as they are
I'd prefer to be arrested

Gateways

I've stopped using the computer
so that's not any issue
and my bank account is empty
so they've clearly been mistaken

as for my reputation
I've lost that long ago
but if he'd got the time to chat
I could tell him of my ailments.

The line goes dead, he's disappeared
it must be something that I've said
a scam, a fraudster I've seen the light
how do these people sleep at night!

Strike

A blow
A last resort
A failure to resolve

Both parties
Battered and bruised
No real winners

A way to show strength
A way to show dissent
To spread the pain

A way to force a deal
By withdrawing labour

By bringing to a standstill

Believing in a just cause
Deepening the rift
Hardening the positions

An open wound
That even when resolved
Will leave a lasting scar

A failure to resolve
A last resort
A blow

UNITY Acrostics

Unless we realise there is
No next time. This
Is the time we have
To make a choice
You and me both

Until the sun is no more and there is
No moon to light the night, then
In this world of hours, of ours
There is just the one home and
You and me, we're all the same

John S. Langley

Lost & Found

'New' Roman remains have been found in Carlisle they are surprisingly complex and extensive.

The building was so full of life
of raucous sound, hot air and
mixed aromas of perfumes, oils
bodies and their sweat

So many people were involved
to cook, to heat, to maintain
in such familiarity of purpose
that everybody knew

So many years of usefulness
until the chaos and havoc of
State level change caused a
decline, the onset of ruin

1,000 years pass, the stone
walls stand, still proud, until
they are mined on an
industrial scale

the little that remains is now
buried although there is still
an aural memory passed on
morphed into myth

Gateways

During the following 500 yrs
the memory fades, no visible
evidence remains, grass now
covers the spot
....

Re-discovered by mistake it
lies more than 1 metre under
the surface, unknown and a
puzzle or riddle now

newly uncovered we marvel
and guess at the little that
survives, a new fascination
like uncovering

a fossilised dinosaur, a relic
sterilised by time, the sights
sounds and smells removed
only bare bones remain

Such do our works live, die
and perhaps see the light
again, though the original
vitality is gone

Is such as this an example
of what is past
or of what is to come?

John S. Langley

Old Knowledge

The pages are over 300 years old
delicate, browning and brittle

Before I can attempt to re-cover
I must stabilise the core

The old glue has turned to crystal
and needs to be removed

I seek out the heart, the pages
black inked, intact, though foxed

As I work, I appreciate the process
each page showing the printer's art

An invisible hand still stretching
across the sands of time

The words are a 'new' translation
from the Latin left behind

What can an old book teach us
when it has been re-spined?

Gateways

After the work is finished
the new glue good and dried

I leaf again through the pages
and read a little of what's there

"For he who grasped the world's exhausted store
Yet never had enough, and wanted more"

I put down the book, a job complete
and wonder if we'll ever learn

What we have known for centuries…

John S. Langley

Standing Stones

Everybody knew
5,000 years ago
what these stones
were for

The monumental effort
the numbers involved
they must have felt
it was worth it

Then the knowing of purpose
crystal clear and passed on
generation to generation
as naturally as breathing

A function as obvious
as churches or mosques
universities, market
places, calendars or…?

But when did it stop?
When did the word
of mouth dry up?
And why?

Gateways

Built to last, they have
outlasted their builders
to leave an insoluble
puzzle

Gazing at these stones
I am lead to ponder
how much of what
everybody knows now

will still be remembered
in 5,000 years time
or would it be better
to be forgotten…?

Antecedents

We know they were here
Because without them we would not be
And because of what they left behind;
in stone, in wood, in ceramics
and in so many other ways

some have bequeathed us their
written word, but what were
they really like? What did they
smell like, what value

did they place on life and death?
How like us were they in their
thoughts and aspirations? I don't
mean the intelligentsia

the wealthy or powerful, I mean
everybody else, the 'commoners'
the vast majority, those whose
ancestral aural legacy

Gateways

is now lost, dissipated into the
ether of time and space. How long
does it take for their ways to fade, for
old lessons to be forgotten?

Do we always need to repeat the
same errors, re-learn the same truths
and wonder who we are?

John S. Langley

Listening to the Ancestors

An old man sits upon a rock
The rock is red, as is his face
in part, painted with pigment
He sits cross-legged, his eyes
are sightless but he sees. He
speaks to anyone who will listen

"When species travel they evolve
adapt to the new environment
the water, or lack of it, the heat
the nature of the land

All creatures are interconnected
with others and with their place
and if they can't change in good
time they cease to be

and others fill the gap until the
limits of life are reached and no
matter how much adaptation
there is it is not enough

Such are the hard facts for most
But we seem to be a little different
We seem to have an ability to a
limited extent

Gateways

to change the environment, make
it more amenable, irrigate the fields
bring water to where we want it
harness fire for warmth

purify the air, fertilise the soil, or
contaminate the water, burn down
cities and rainforests, poison the air
denude the soil

Our ability is limited, how will we use it?"

An old man sits upon a rock
The rock is red, as is his face
in part, painted with pigment
He sits cross-legged, his eyes
are sightless but he sees. He
speaks to anyone who will listen.
The Sun is going down.
Setting red.

Darn

When I was a lad
in the Megalithic
socks with holes
were darned

Not thrown away

Trousers, jackets
jumpers, shirts
were patched

Not thrown away

Shoes, watches
glasses, were
repaired

Not thrown away

You did not get
a completely new
outfit

but were renewed
in parts, if you were
lucky

Gateways

And if you grew out
of something it was
passed on

Not thrown away

So that somebody
else could have the
benefit

But sad to say
this time is gone now

Thrown away

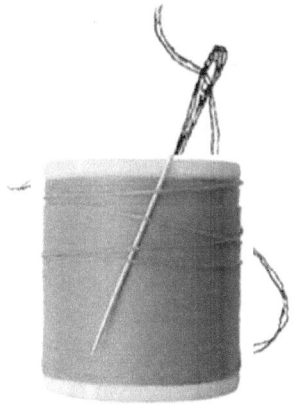

John S. Langley

What if

What if the Neanderthal
(our name for them)
were not less intelligent
but more creative
than Homo sapiens
(our name for us)

What if the real difference
was that they lived off
the land, and ate more
greens and fruit, while
we took to meat, and
needed weapons

to hunt and kill. What if
they were kinder to their
environment, painted
what they held dear on
cave walls, left hand-
prints behind

Gateways

What if the 2% in our
DNA signals a kind of
co-existence. What if
it were simply better
weapons that won us
the premier spot

What if they were
gentle creatures that we
drove to extinction not
through greater intelligence
but brute strength
ours the kind of persona
that we bequeath to them

What if we are the Neanderthals?

John S. Langley

Carnivorous

To all us carnivores;
does the separation
from the raising, the
slaughtering and the
butchering make us
feel more humane?

It's a thing we don't
like to talk about in
our 'civilised' neck
of the woods but in
lots of other parts of
the world it's the norm

I like to eat meat but
don't like killing things
How does that work?
I do something else
and buy my meat
packaged & prepared
by somebody else

Gateways

There is something in
my psyche that means
I automatically switch
from a feeling of empathy
for animals that inhabit
the land alive and well

to enjoying the taste
of lamb, beef, chicken, pork.
Although I wouldn't
like the thought of anything
eating me!

I've been born a hypocrite!
At least I admit it.

John S. Langley

Layers

The Earth
absorbs memories
lays down history
raises seabeds
to mountain tops

Today
we stand on top
slowly sinking
ready to be part
of yesterday

Best make
the most of it
I was never
a real fan
of Geology

Gateways

The Naming of Parts

A name
An identity bestowed
With no permission

An aid
To communication
That becomes

Misconstrued
As a mark
Of ownership

A flag planted
A territory taken
It is

As senseless
As believing
That a cloud

Can be fenced
Or the Earth bought
And paid for.

A Bird Fable

A Rook and a Pheasant fighting over seeds
each one wanting what the other one needs
Two birds together with just one thought
to fight off the other one with everything they've got

A Rook and a Pheasant each one going for the other
Fighting over seeds I don't know why they bother
Two birds swapping pecks neither giving way
Until they got fed up and both of them flew away

Seeds scattered all about, a tasty little bit
Down came a chaffinch and a dainty little Tit
Both ignored the other, too intent on making hay
Eating up all the seeds, it was their lucky day

Pylons

Pylons stride across the moors
metal caged and strung with progress
an electrical impulse thoroughfare
braving all weathers carrying power

distributing the means to light
and heat and cook and create and
communicate, too easy to ignore

such a commonplace sight
the changed landscape of metal trees
and wires an accepted norm for
most of us a mark we've made

a price we've had to pay.

John S. Langley

The Trouble with Parts

We break things into parts
To simplify is to understand
Physics, biology, chemistry
Geology and so on…
Each throwing bricks
at the other when blame
needs to be apportioned

Backing their own claims
with sharpened equations
repeatable empirical results
peer assessed, published
in reputable journals with
worldwide circulation
meaning they must be right
in their intellectual fight
that has no end…

Meanwhile Nature has great
power but no responsibility
Not even over it's name;
natura, natur, naturaleza
ziran, priroda, luonto, natuur
asili, kudarata, nadur, imvelo
dabeecadda, thrrmchati
and so on…

Gateways

When will we understand
there are no neat components
only a whole too complex
for us to grasp, a world full
of unforeseen consequences
which is the only surety in an
ever changing universe

We would be better to maintain
the environment we've got
sustain the 'as is' for as long
as possible, don't be too clever
consult the hitchhiker's guide

'Don't Panic!'
The answer is 42.

John S. Langley

AI

There was a time
when poetry was
written with pen
and ink or typed
by human hand

When books were
plotted by beings
unreliable mammals
characters that did
not work 24/7 but

took a break to sleep
but we have seen the
light. Now it is much
simpler - and here is
the result.

Gateways

What's in a Name
(Bluetooth)

What would Harald think
(though he is hardly likely
to find out) that his name
(a salacious nickname
probably referring to poor
dental work) has been
appropriated more than
one thousand years later
(though he would have been
familiar with the idea of
appropriation) as a symbol
of unification and connectivity
(though his then method of
unification was more bloody)
and that his initials blended
in runic form (would he have
been able to decipher their
meaning?) is now common
parlance around the world.
Would he be proud or
would he wish that he'd got
his tooth fixed?

John S. Langley

No-Brainer

Getting power direct
from the Sun and
wind and water
rather than releasing
stored up sunshine
from fossil fuels
that tips the balance
against us has got to
be one of the easiest
choices that face
Homo sapiens

who have the means
and can communicate
with each other
around the globe.
So how ridiculous
for convoluted
Capitalist, political
or local interests
to get in the way
and stop us doing
the blindingly obvious

It's like shifting around
the deckchairs
on the Titanic.

Gateways

Seeing is Believing?

The old oak bows
It's green leaves chatter
Driven by the unseen

A field becomes a sea
Grass waves undulate
Sounds like rushing water

And I am pushed or bent
As I feel the presence
Of the invisible force

All that is seen is believed
But the unseen is no less true
Though our eyes are useless

The old oak bows
The field becomes a sea
And only if I am there

And not elsewhere
Can I feel the presence
And begin to understand

John S. Langley

Changes

A new season of winds and storms
Has replaced the bitter cold of snow
That I remember from my youth

The snow came in November
December, stayed til February
Some years it lay more thickly

Than others, but it would come
Cause disruption, the roads icy
But now we may not get snow

Now we get a Windy season
Bringing down trees, tearing
Off roofs, and rains so heavy

That 100 year floods are now
Regular events. I didn't think
I'd ever say it, but I'm nostalgic

For those other Winters!

Categorisation

We believe we can
Organize Nature
through categorisation
Like butterflies
pinned in a box
wings held open
kept in a drawer
under proper conditions
for use as reference
or for research
a typical specimen
of the species

———————

You should not be here!
Your brown spotted wings
Yellow ringed faux eyes
To ogle and deter

You are too far North!
It is warmer winds
That have carried you here
A Speckled Wood

John S. Langley

A new entrant to our patch!
Sitting for a second
Like the place is yours
Before flitting out of reach

But I nailed you!
The iPhone captured
an image, good enough
to look up and confirm

Your name, your foolishness
In venturing here, I file the
photo, your wings spread wide
and must share on Facebook

Filed forever
Liked or commented on
For a much shorter time
You are not static!

Gateways

Not pinned, or nailed
Or kept in place
How dare you annoy us
With your adaptability

Do you not realise
We must now redraw
The maps, amend books
How unthoughtful of you

To we who have done you no harm
But would like to finish classifying
Naming and placing everything
In a constantly changing world

Maybe we should rethink
our approach to knowledge?

John S. Langley

The Missing Element

The ancients had it right
with their four states of matter
Soil for solid
Air for gas
Water for liquid
Fire for plasma

Somewhere along the way
perhaps with the Periodic Table
or Boyle's Law
we've lost one
though it's there
all around us

From the 'stable' state of the Sun
to every fire we light
or witness
Plasma
it's doesn't get
it's due attention

Maybe it should.

Gateways

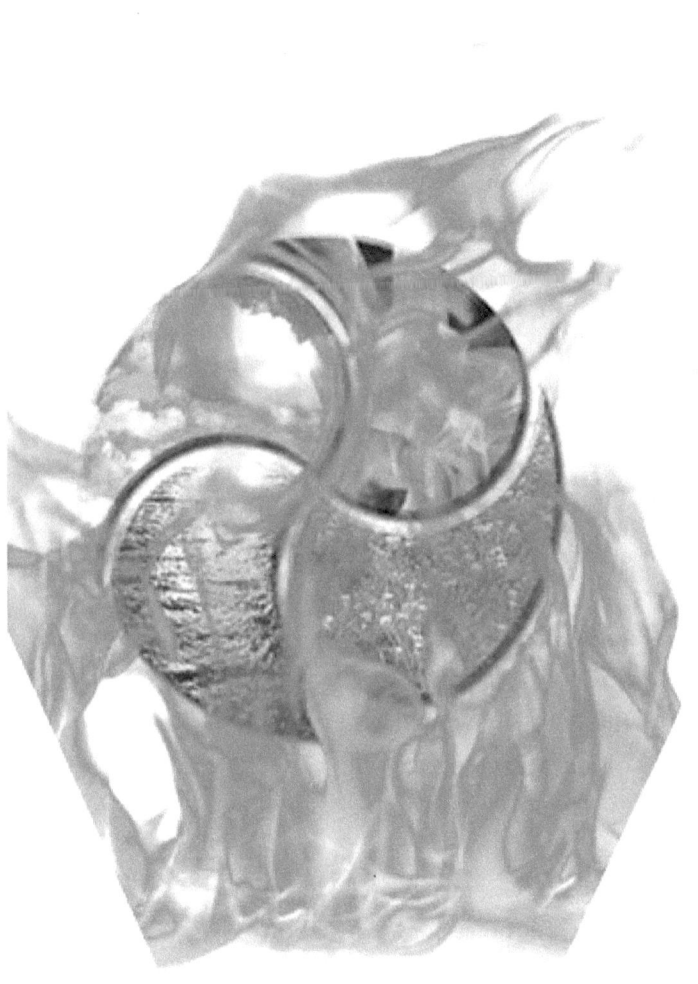

John S. Langley

Going Extinct

They've found Woolly Mammoth bones
locked underground for 50,000 years
preserved in a peat bog

That's not so long ago. Considering
the Earth is 4.5 billion years old
we've only just missed them

though they do believe our ancestors
lived alongside them, hunted them
ate their flesh, used their skins

to keep out the cold. I wonder what
the last Woolly Mammoth thought
before it died. Was it alone

hidden from view, stuck in a bog
or still with its calf trying to suck
on an empty teat?

Now, I guess, we would try and
preserve the last few, in a zoo
or a National Park

Gateways

After so many years of existence
in harmony with their surroundings
it must have been a surprise

Did we or our like finish them off
too big a target to miss, too
cumbersome to run?

Or was it climate, environment
or disease that reduced the herds
then weakened by inbreeding?

And when it's our turn, what will
it be? Will we believe it or will we
sink into the bog with a look of
surprise on our faces…

John S. Langley

Up in Smoke

When the flames were gone
And the fire cooled
There were no words left
Only ashes

Climate Crisis
(what Climate Crisis?)

It's like we're sitting
Onboard the Titanic
In one of the saloons
Somebody is asking

Concern on their face
'Iceberg? Did anyone
Hear anything about
Some kind of iceberg?'

'Not me,' replies one
'Felt a bit of a bump,'
Says another. They
Call over the waiter

Who arrives and asks
'Would you like one
More gin and tonic?'
'Oh, yes,' they all say.

John S. Langley

Mutual Dependence

Yes, do go into the forest.

Not at night when ancient fear
sparks a flight or fright
response

But in the day when green
shade shines down
a blessing

And pools of light mottle
sight and scene
in clean air

That carries common scents
remembered remnants
in our genes

Relax in the familiar, refresh
your human soul
Be still

Gateways

If we remember where we're from
remember it's here
we belong

Perhaps we'd value it the more
amidst oxygen-producing
trees

Feeding on each other's
exhalations

John S. Langley

The Problem Was

The problem was
That we couldn't afford
to save the world

We had the technology
We had the need
but not the money

We had the materials
We had the expertise
but not the will

I know it seems daft now
I know you can't eat cash
it was the way we did things

Balance the books, don't
Print money, covet it
it's all important

We thought about it a lot
Actually agreed what we
should be doing

But the numbers didn't
Work, there just weren't
enough coins or counters

So we didn't do what we
Knew we had to do and
now it's far too late

How did we allow this to
Happen? If only we could
have our time again…

Gateways

John S. Langley

The Difference

For most of our fellow animals
a good day is surviving and
being well-fed. They know no
more, ask no more and can do
no more

If their world changes they
must change with it or move
to another place if they can
and if they can't they
disappear

They cannot influence the
outcome beyond how they
naturally interact with other
species and their immediate
surroundings

Such animals cannot be held
responsible for something
they have no knowledge of.
Only those who know and are
capable can be blamed

for not doing enough.

Lost Cause?

It's always worth
chasing down
a lost cause

A certain boundary
when it leaves
the bat

But the ball slows
as it sweeps
across

The green baize
of the outfield
is chased

Down, gained upon
fingers stretching
hand cupping

Scooping
the ball back
while the body rolls

John S. Langley

Over the boundary marker
a teammate bends
bows to collect

Throws it back
into safe gloves
the crowd applaud

Two runs scored
Two runs saved
Honours even

Game on !

A lost cause
an impossible chase
not lost and
not impossible…

NATURALLY SPEAKING

John S. Langley

Fleur de Leaf

(The Fleur-de-Lis has many symbolic uses mainly associated with Reverence, Light and Life. This poem takes a slant-eyed view from a real observation on a frosty morning's walk.)

Frosted leaves
Winter bitten
Hard edged

An evergreen turned white
Bristles with stalagmites
Sharp as an old man's beard

Refracts
A low Sun's
Orange-yellow richness

With a glass-like fragility
Twixt life and death
An ancient-modern symbol

of lost youth
of our Summer over

or stands in anticipation
of a new Spring

Gateways

John S. Langley

The Best Laid Plans

So I spun this web, see
my spinnerets spreading silken threads
me hanging, swaying, joining the dots
creating my own deadly work of art
an invisible net of sticky strands

Then I retreated into a corner
still legs spread out, feeling the tension
waiting for the twang of startled capture
So I could scuttle out quickly spin a
a tight cocoon, my own version
of a food cupboard

That was the plan but I'm not a weatherman
I knew it was getting colder and almost froze
but I'm an arachnid, so I would survive
What I didn't foresee was the winter frost
clinging like white filings to my handiwork

From my position I don't get a fly-sized view
But I could guess what it looked like
No longer invisible, quite the opposite
May as well have written a sign
'Danger! Keep away!'

Gateways

So now there's no alternative
but to sit tight and wait it out
listening to my stomach rumble
and hoping for a thaw.

John S. Langley

Spring Yellow

Yellow is the colour of April
Emergent blooms that shine in the Sun
Light up the pathways, edges and fields
Lounge on the slopes of the river banks
Open in their newness, swaying and growing
Winter is gone, they cry

Yellow is the colour of Spring

First Apples

First apples on a new tree
Planted four years ago
Or was it five?
Eating apples
Good for pies
Or crumbles
Blushing red
as I talk about them

Go Sloe

The sloes are ready for picking
The flexible feel of ripeness
The powdery purple to blue
Convince us to brave the thorns
Needle length, needle sharp
Beckoning unwary fingertips
To add pain to this gathering
As it's collected, de-stalked
Then later sorted, pricked
sugared and ginned

And now we must wait
Watch the colour develop
And look forward to enjoy
This season's harvest

Blackberries

The blackberries are good
this year
The best for some time

We don't know why but
are happy
to take full advantage

The fruit is soft and
easy picking
if you avoid the thorns

We eat some as we go
naturally sweet
staining our fingers

Jams and crumbles await
in the future
from this unexpected boon

John S. Langley

Evidence

There's hedgehog poo
in the garden

Like a black slug frozen
on the grass

Full of the inedible remains
of insects and worms

I looked, I dissected
it's true

Now we must look out
for the prickles

Jumping with fleas
the snorting in the verges

You can't hide
We know you're there!

Gateways

A New Perspective

We have a new App !
It identifies birds by their song
It's amazing

We sit quietly for 2 minutes
Listening to the sounds, watching
The App do its work

Today the birds identified were:
Swallow, Sparrow, Treecreeper,
Great Spotted Woodpecker

Robin, Siskin, Crow, Pheasant
And Blue Tit! We've never stopped
To listen before

It makes you think - what else
Are we oblivious to as we go on
Our busy way?

And - if so many different birds
Can share the same air space
Without damaging it
                      - then why can't we?

John S. Langley

Windhover

A kestrel hangs high
on nothing
suspended
by hard work
it's body still
eyes focused
listening
poised
sensing movement

Then down it plunges
talons leading
daggers drawn
hits the ground
delivers a fatal shock
and lifts
muscles straining
wings open
up, up and up
regaining height
grasping fur
a small body
tightly held

That's all I see
before it disappears
to I know not where
a dot in the distance
a welcome comma
to my day.

Dragonfly

Dragonflies on prismatic wings
dart across the garden
flashing rainbow light
determined in their flight

They look alien to our sight
these prehistoric things
and yet they are at least
as much at home
as you or I

John S. Langley

And Away…

The swallows are going mad today
mid-September and they're getting ready…

Lining the wires
Calling
Churring
Clicking
Circling
Consulting their maps

Feeding in a frenzy
Feasting on flies
Forming groups
Spreading wings
Testing strength
In swoops and turns

A long journey in prospect
hoping for helpful winds
to lift their wings
and take them South

More swallows
than we've seen all year
it's been a fallow time
for our nesting pairs

Gateways

This "Summer's" weather did not help
the sun saw them in and sees them out

But in between when it really mattered
the sky cried too often to a watery Sun

Now it's time for them all to leave again
To take up the elemental challenge again

We can only say farewell
And wish them well upon their way
And hope we'll see them back again

John S. Langley

The Hawthorn Ridge

Gnarled and twisted
are the sinews of the hawthorn stem
grow from sparse soil
seeking purchase and sustenance
through their toughened roots
hardened by seasons of perpetual change

And still they survive to blossom
fresh white in the sunshine
inviting new bees into the flowers' core
their to feed and carry off a part
of their future selves
that must settle in some foreign heart

and swell to an autumnal maturity
berries red as poppy petals tempting
the hungry wings that have returned
from cooler climes to feast upon
this bounty, then digest and free the
seed in haphazard fashion

Gateways

And for a few a new generation takes
hold, unconscious of their genesis
their future bound in genes
forged through time, passed to them
to pass to others while unknowing
parents struggle on the Hawthorn ridge

Their stems are twisted like old rope
grotesque beneath the leather green
of new leaves and buds of blossom
facing into the wind and rain waiting
for the Sun to signal the right time to
begin again…

Empty Hive

The bees have struggled this year
A summer swarm taking residence
in an empty hive

They made themselves at home
Found pollen for a new generation
white, yellow, orange and red

But the weather was not kind
Too few flowers, too few flying days
weakened the colony

After so much effort to survive
they needed a helping hand from
pats of sugar fondant

Which they immediately took in
I hope it helped, time (and Winter)
will tell the rest.

Gateways

A Trifling Imperative

Ancient roots breed new life
Leaves, buds, flowers, fruit

On such bounty others feed
Raising a new generation

Spreading seeds that seek
Fertile soils to nest within

Ripe for shoots to sprout
At the right time of year

And, with luck and vitality
To grow and to survive

Among the fallen leaves
The decaying petals

Probing, forging new roots
And, with increasing maturity

To breed it's own new life
Leaves, buds, flowers, fruit.

Green Man?

This Green Man is not green
he's been hidden inside
this wood for so long

Waiting to be uncovered
by the artist's hand and
tooled to face us

in 3D, bearded and aged
Was he always there? And
where is the Green Woman?

Has every tree a soul that
we destroy in order to see?
This Green Man is not green

he should be heard not seen
whispering out of symbiosis
willing to be a go-between

Gateways

John S. Langley

The Right Thing?

A deer carcass found in the garden
the cause of its demise unknown
we decide to leave it to nature and
over days, weeks we see mammals
birds, insects take each their part
leaving bare bones to submerge
beneath grasses and vegetation

Were we wrong to leave it?
Should we have intervened to 'rescue'
the body, to bury or burn the remains
as a salve to our own sensibilities
and not allow the gradual gory decay
a consumption, a distribution of wealth
an eventual disappearance?

It was an accidental death
that benefited many
was that wrong?

Fireflies

The first time I saw fireflies I freaked out
We were in a rondavel in Hluhluwe Game
Reserve in Natal, South Africa. It was night
we were asleep, the sounds of the bush
woke us up. There were flashing pinpoints
of light at the end of the bed; yellow, blue
red. I didn't know what was going on, so I
did what came naturally, I screamed.

I have to say that screaming at fireflies
makes little difference and once I'd settled
down we watched the light show in awe
wondering how such fluorescent fireworks
could be so bright, what they meant and
what they were communicating. Once our
fear had subsided, interest and joy took its
place; such is the hierarchy of responses.

John S. Langley

Perspectives

When I first took a drop of pond water
put it on a glass slide and peered at it
through a microscope I saw, floating as
if in space, a green sphere containing
other green spheres

I learned that this was the Volvox algae
a spherical colony of some 50,000 cells
I thought it a miracle then and wondered
what other marvels there might be hidden
from the naked eye

Years later I looked at a photo of the Earth
looking back from the perspective of the
planet Neptune, about 2.8 billion miles away
It was a pale blue dot, no bigger than the
Volvox had appeared in the water.

Gateways

Home?

We find an African waterhole
the noise of our own engine
fills our ears, masking reality

We stop. The air conditioning
remains on. It is too hot with
the windows up in our tin can

We wind down the two front
windows. Half way. You only
live once! We'll keep a watch

We are not of this place but
feel a part, though separated
inside our mechanical capsule

We sit and watch and listen
There is no background music
There is no live commentary

There is a quiet, peppered with
the calls of birds the splashing
of water, the snorting of Hippos

John S. Langley

It is flat. Grasslands punctuated
with Acacia trees, oases of shade
Zebra and Giraffe come to drink

bending or sinking to their knees
bowing heads to the life giving
liquid. And an Elephant farts, it's

aroma pulsing through our open
windows, assaulting our senses
You don't get this on the TV !

We do not get out, we're not that
stupid! This is as close as we are
ever likely to get, and yet it feels

somehow familiar. We could not
survive here, have not the ability
have lost the knack.

I envy those who can.

Gateways

John S. Langley

Gateways

A FEW MORE

John S. Langley

Posser

Essential once
A relic now
How times
Have changed

Sought after
It's value high
Supply limited
No longer

And today?
Which of
What we value
Will pass the test
Of time

Proggy Mat

In the industrial homes of the workers of the North East of England the making of 'proggy mats', by recycling otherwise wasted pieces of fabric, was a common and acquired skill. The resulting floor coverings were welcomed for their comfort, their vibrant colours, their warmth and for being hardwearing, not unlike their makers.

My back is an old hessian sack
backbone and still ink-marked
for grain

Through this has been poked
over many hours, in poor light
rag strips

I am unique, made with love
to be trodden on, underfoot
hardwearing

Like my makers, who are gone
but live on in me, fine women
one and all.

John S. Langley

Tankard

This pewter tankard has travelled
from Newcastle to Northumberland
excise stamped in recognition
VR71, GR503 and the 'Castle' mark

It's the volume that's important here
One Imperial Pint checked annually
to give the consumer confidence
in their consumption of the many

gallons of local beer that have passed
through here, one pint at a time from
barrel to throat in the years 1892
to 1935

The Authorities sought to ensure that
none of the many hands that held this
pot have been cheated of drops or
portions of farthings

What has it seen? It's keeps it's council
and stands, still here, ready to do its job
if called upon to fulfil its legal duty.
It is empty now but steeped in history.

Gateways

John S. Langley

Orkney Chair

A remnant of the Age of Straw
when Orcadians creatively used
this wonder material for mats
and roofs, ropes and baskets
of all sizes.

Driftwood, black-oat straw and
the long strong grass called 'bent'
were then the base materials for
making chairs

Handcrafted to individual design
utilitarian against the draughts
until a new use is defined, a set
of four outlined

A success in Victorian times, then
a decline to abandonment. Revived
again after World War 2 as a different
thing altogether

Now a sophisticated piece, prime oak
instead of driftwood, naturally fumed
and finished with raw linseed oil and
made to last generations

Gateways

We saw these being made during a
visit, met the man at his craft, started
to understand what it really meant, it
is not only a chair

A tradition, a symbol, a pride in history
and craftsmanship. We could not afford
one then, with three young children in
need of feeding

Thirty years later we visited an Antiques
Fair in Hexham, and surprisingly see
an Orkney Chair, awakening memories
a fine example

Now it stands in our home, a reminder
of a heritage, a history, and traditional
craftsmanship kept alive, of times
long gone, but fondly brought to mind.

John S. Langley

Loch Ness

Middle distance mountains
heather covered, bracken brown
mists lying like a woollen blanket
in the invisible valleys

In the foreground there is a track
cart-worn and rutted, and trees
that are bent skew-whiff by winds
invisible to the eye

On the edge of the track there is
a single figure, a woman, clothed
for her time, signalling a history
her now, now past

And in the midst there is the loch
serene and still over deep waters
A frozen scene in oils, and time
held behind glass, framed

An artist's work, the skill to capture
a moment, fleeting yet everlasting
Nature's majesty and our small place.
I see no monsters here.

Gateways

John S. Langley

Hills

The low cloud looms like a grey fleece
Is this the sky falling on our heads?
Has the old prediction come true
at last?

Moisture caresses the tops of the hills
wisping amongst the green and brown
frail, slight and fleeting yet a powerful
reminder

We travel beneath this mottled roof
covered by a dismal darkening sky
and wonder if a storm will break or
we'll escape

There is a pass, worn by ice and water
that cuts through these hills, we go there
there is light on the other side, the sky
is higher there

19th Century Explorer

Cooped up
in a sailing ship
exploring
new waters

No wonder
tempers frayed
too close the
proximity of egos

Starting off
as colleagues
mutual respect
then tested

Even animosity
does not prevent
the work from
being done

And if you
make it home
you do not need
to see one another

ever again
Except perhaps
in polite
society.

John S. Langley

Trains

Travelling by train, on your own
can put you into a kind of stup-
or. Looking out of the window o-
nly is a distraction, for so long.

People watching can sometim-
es help, earwigging conversa-
tions that should not be listen-
ed into nor spoken out so loudly.

The journey itself can seem end-
less, no book or activity can sp-
eed the clock and then there are
the prospect of delays ...

Travelling with someone else how-
ever, someone you like to be with
is a dream, the talk flows along as
the train rolls smoothly over the rails

The journey seems over before it's
begun, delays would be welcomed
to extend the event, there was too
much to talk about so little time

there's much to look forward to
on the way back.

Gateways

Never the Right Weather

You want a bit of hot sun
But not when you're doing a run

Your garden needs the rain
But not again and again

The snow is visually charming
But you find the cold alarming

You find fog quite mysterious
But getting lost can be serious

Clouds can look nice and fluffy
But at night just get in the way

Of looking for stars and planets
That cause you to get out the blankets

Is there never any ideal weather
Or just the wrong type of clothes

Or a poem that does not always rhyme
Certainly, not all of the time

Though still a poem that can be read
In any sort of weather…

John S. Langley

The Hubble Universe

It took almost 20 years
to put a faulty telescope
into space

Orbiting 350miles up
less than from London
to Edinburgh

Size of a bus, 5,000
orbits a year, each less
than 2hrs

The blurring error
took 3yrs of ingenuity
to solve it

Recaptured by the Space
Shuttle, new parts exchanged
for old

Now, without the obscuring
atmosphere we look further
see more

And the more we see the
smaller we are, the less
significant

Gateways

Near planets, supernova
remnants, star forming
areas

Galaxies, deeper and
further back in time
Old light still shining

Cloud Cuckoo Land

The Greeks
2,500 years ago
laughed at the idea
of asking the birds
to build a land in air
between gods and man
a perfect position
to intercede in both
directions

Maybe it was pie in
the sky, or building
castles in the air but
such a fantastical or
utopian or comical
image remains as
allegory, or metaphor
and still has its uses
to this day

Green

The Egyptian colour of regeneration and rebirth
To the Greeks blue and green were the same !
The colour of the Roman Goddess Venus
of vegetables and vineyards
of merchants and bankers
of gentry in the Renaissance
like the Mona Lisa

The colour of the Romantic movement
of the environmental movement
of permission
of nature, of life
of springtime, of freshness
of youth and inexperience
of emotions from calmness to envy

And all the shades and tones; Celadon
Lime, Fern, Emerald, Malachite, Moss
Sage, Juniper, Chartreuse, Olive, Pear Shamrock,
Seafoam, Pine, Parakeet, Mint, Seaweed, Pickle,
Pistachio, Basil, Crocodile, Apple, Jungle, Mantis
and Jade… to name but a few

And all I wanted to do
was to write a new poem about green
    I mean…
               …what chance did I stand?

John S. Langley

Inking

This poem is loosely based on an anecdote told by the brilliant graphic novel illustrator Dave Gibbons at the 'Lakes International Comic Arts Festival' held in Bowness-on-Windermere 29th September-1st October 2023.

The pencil sketch arrives
drops on the mat like
a leaf falling

I pick it up carefully
open it in anticipation
and am not

disappointed. The line
is exquisite, the detail
and texture

show the hand of a
true draughtsman and
skilled artist

I have been asked to
ink it, something I do
with trepidation

Gateways

First I must decide if
I should ink the original
or make a copy

With respect there is
only one answer and
I take up my pens

Follow the artist's lead
line and then shade
carefully

Finally I breathe, step
away and am content
with what I've done

When the ink it dry
I go over it with an
eraser, removing

the last vestiges of
the original pencil
marks and brush

away the resulting
crumbs. Now all the
original is gone

John S. Langley

either hidden under
the imposed ink or
lying at my feet

Where now is the
artist's hand? I have
done what I

was asked. Was it an
act of destruction
or refinement

a necessary step
in the production
process. After

that someone else
would colour and letter
in order to

arrive at a final image
that could be
reproduced

millions of times. I put
away my pens. The art-
work though gone

Gateways

would be attributed to
the artist, would be part
of a lasting legacy

remembered long after
the one who did the inking
has been forgotten.

It Would Have Been Superb!

I had an idea
for a poem
now
my mind has gone blank

All I remember
is just how
good
it was going to be

The best idea
I've had in
ages
just needing to be written

But now it has gone
flown away on butterfly
wings
into a library of lost things

One more to all the things
I thought I'd do
someday
but have forgotten about.

www.ingramcontent.com/pod-product-compliance
Lightning Source LLC
Chambersburg PA
CBHW021103080526
44587CB00010B/351